Jackson★Five

text   **Charles and Ann Morse**
illustrations   **John Keely**
design concept **Mark Landkamer**

published by **Creative Education**
              Mankato, Minnesota

Published by Creative Educational Society, Inc.,
123 South Broad Street, Mankato, Minnesota 56001
Copyright © 1975 by Creative Educational Society, Inc. International
copyrights reserved in all countries.
No part of this book may be reproduced in any form without written permission
from the publisher. Printed in the United States.
Distributed by Childrens Press, 1224 West Van Buren Street, Chicago, Illinois 60607
Library of Congress Numbers: 74-12248 ISBN: 0-87191-389-5
Library of Congress Cataloging in Publication Data
Morse, Charles.   Jackson Five.
SUMMARY: Traces the Jackson Five's rise to fame, describes their
family life, and gives a brief biography of each of the five stars.
1. Jackson 5 (Musical group)—Juvenile literature.
[1. Jackson 5 (Musical group) 2. Musicians. 3. Negroes—Biography]
I. Morse, Ann, joint author. II. Keely, John, illus. III. Title.
ML3930.J3M67   784'.092'2 [B] [920]   74-12248
ISBN 0-87191-389-5

"I'm goin' back to Indiana," lead singer Michael Jackson's voice could be heard above the others. "Back to where I started from. Goin' back to Indiana. Indiana, here I come." This hit song of 1970 became real for the Jackson Five early in 1971.

It was Jackson Five Day in Gary, Indiana, a cold January 31. Though the temperature was low, it was a day of high spirits.

Plans for the day were as blustery as the 40 MPH winds that blew through the streets of Gary that day. Mayor Richard Hatcher and the other planners of the Jackson Five Day watched the film crew buzz around getting lights set up.

The Jackson Five were to come into the city by helicopter. Then they would be paraded to their old house at 23rd and Jackson Streets. The mayor was going to name the block, "Jackson 5 Street" for the week and lay a cornerstone in front of the home where all the Jackson children were born. Big plans, they were, for a very special day.

"Goin' back to Indiana. Indiana, here I come."

The winds won over those plans, cancelling the helicopter drop-in, the parade and the cornerstone ceremony. Instead, the festivities began at City Hall.

In less than 10 minutes City Hall was filled with hundreds of children. Behind the mayor sat 12 teen-agers in the chairs of the council members.

"Behind me are the winners of the Jackson Five poster contest and essay contest," Mayor Hatcher said

Going Back to Indiana

7

as he welcomed everyone. The mayor and the audience looked around at the posters on the walls. The theme was hope and encouragement for youth, "You Can Make It If You Try."

"Each winning student will receive a prize," Mayor Hatcher went on. "They will be able to have their pictures taken with the Jackson Five."

Finally the moment came that all had been waiting for. Kids stood on their chairs, leaned out into the aisles and turned, craning their necks to see the Jackson Five come walking toward the mayor. The Jackson brothers met the contest winners and shook hands with each of them. Cheers went up from the audience as Michael and Tito exchanged power shakes with some of the winners who offered their hands for the grip.

Joe Jackson, their father, stepped up to the microphone to say thank you. "Lay it on, Jackson," his sons cheered, "lay it on."

Then came the awards. The Jackson Five accepted them easily and gracefully. A congressman gave the young stars a flag which had once flown above the state capitol. They received a plaque from Indiana University for "inspiring hope for the young." Mayor Hatcher gave the Jackson Five the keys to the city, saying, "I'm proud today that the Jackson Five have carried the name of Gary throughout the country and the world, and made it a name to be proud of."

"I'm comin' home now . . . I still got Indiana goin' with me."

Each of the Jackson brothers said a few words; and Tito put it all together with, "We're glad to be home. There's no place like home."

After City Hall, the Jackson Five were whisked away

8

to West Side High School for their first concert at 3 pm. Then the mayor took the Jackson family to his home for a small private party. The Jacksons and Mayor Hatcher have been friends for many years. All the Jackson kids played little league baseball, and Hatcher always supported the kids' teams. Katherine and Joe Jackson, the Five's parents, had often worked on Hatcher's election campaigns.

After the Jackson Five performed at the evening concert, their limousines were waiting to take them to another party in Gary. Joe Jackson's relatives had been preparing food for days for a Jackson family reunion. All evening long aunts, uncles, cousins and sisters arrived to help eat the sweet potato pies, fried chicken, black-eyed peas and salads.

After eating, many of the Jacksons settled down to play Tonk, a card game, with their famous relatives. When one or all of the Jackson Five were interrupted time and time again for a photograph or autograph, they showed no irritation. The young stars were learning to be genuine professionals.

The Jackson Five went back to Indiana where they started from — five warm, genuine kids, five professional stars.

Eight and a half months later the Jackson Five did their first television special, called "Going Back to Indiana." Some of the stars that appeared as guests were Tom Smothers, Bill Cosby, Bill Russell and Rosey Grier.

The Jackson Five's own interests were the central themes of the show — baseball, racing cars, basketball and, of course, music. The highlight of the hour-long show was the actual concert performance that the Jackson Five had done in their home state.

In 1969 another very special day occurred in Gary, Indiana, a day which has come to mean as much to the Jackson Five as the day of "Going back to Indiana." It was the day in April when the people of Gary celebrate the birthday of their home town.

Mayor Hatcher had lined up some stars to entertain the people of Gary in an outdoor concert. Diana Ross and the Supremes were to be the highlight of the concert. Of course the mayor made sure that the town's favorite musical group, the Jackson Five, were to perform, too; but this was before the Jackson Five were known outside Gary.

Mayor Hatcher had planned the concert as a benefit to help his election campaign. The Five were a little nervous, knowing there would be many people watching.

It was noon. The Jackson Five prepared for the concert. Jackie wore a bright shirt and a new pair of bells; Tito slipped on his purple sweater; Jermaine chose purple, too; Marlon crawled into a yellow sweater, and Michael decided on a bright shirt and gold bells.

The whole Jackson family climbed into their VW bus and headed toward the park. It was time for the concert to begin. Joe Jackson, Tito, Jackie and Jermaine rearranged equipment. Jermaine and Tito plugged in their guitars. Ronnie Rancifer and Johnny Jackson, the Jackson Five's cousins, set up the electric piano and drums.

The cousins played back-up for the Five. In minutes, Tito and Jermaine's guitars strummed the Jackson Five into their first number. The Jackson Five tore through songs, giving each one all they had. "More!" "Fantastic!" "Great!" The crowd was jumping with enthusiasm.

Pushing through the crowd to the foot of the stage completely unnoticed in all the excitement, was Gary's

Discovery Day

mayor, and with him none other than Diana Ross! Diana was rocking back and forth, clapping her hands and saying, "Right on!" with the rest of the crowd.

The mayor was smiling and moving in time to the music. "See, Diana? These kids are great . . . !" the mayor shouted above the J-5 sounds; but Diana didn't need to be told; she was sold!

When their numbers were over, the Jackson Five smiled at the applause, waved and ran right for the bus. They were shy but happy about their performance. "Let's go; let's get out of here!" they said to their dad.

Before they could pull away from their parking spot, a voice called to them, "Don't go, Mr. Jackson; don't go!" The Jackson family looked. Their mouths dropped open. Who should be calling and running toward the bus but the mayor and Diana Ross herself.

Joe Jackson stepped out of the bus, and the boys rolled down their windows. It was hard to believe what the mayor, Diana Ross and their dad were talking about. Diana wanted the Jackson Five to come to Detroit, to Motown Records and meet its president, Berry Gordy, Jr.

It was discovery day that April day in 1969. From that moment on, the Jackson Five moved into the world of professional musicians.

The Jackson Five went to Chicago where they performed for Berry Gordy, then on to Detroit where the boys and their father signed a contract with Motown. It was a dream come true, to be part of the Motown family. Other Motowners included some of the Five's favorites: The Temptations, Stevie Wonder, the Miracles and many more, including, of course, Diana Ross and the Supremes.

Diana had taken the Jackson Five under her wing.

At many of her concerts the J-5 would perform with her. Their first album was entitled, *Diana Ross Presents The Jackson Five.* It included a couple of their hit singles, "I Want You Back" and "Stand."

Because of their hit records, it wasn't long before the Jackson Five were filling every seat at their own concerts. The J-5 drew instant response from pre-teen and early teen-agers. Sometimes their sound is called "bubblegum soul." Basically, their music is rhythm and blues.

The back-up sounds vary. Motown's sophisticated arrangers put funky sounds, early 1950 sounds and jazz sounds behind their singing. "ABC" is straight rock and roll with its choppy, clipped lyrics. "I'll Be There" and "What Love You Save" are two more of their first hits. Both swing between Michael's lead falsetto to the harmonies of the brothers' voices and back to Michael's. One magazine reporter called it music "propelled by a cleanly energetic rhythm."

Tony Jones, the group's road manager, says the Jackson Five are six-dimensional — each is an individual, and yet they all work together as a group.

[1]"How Diana Ross Discovered the Jackson Five!," *TcB!,* Vol 1, No. 1. Spring, 1971.

The Jacksons

The Jackson family is a tight-knit, sensitive, real family; the parents, Joe and Katherine Jackson, have seen to that.

All of Mr. and Mrs. Jackson's 9 children were born in Gary and lived in the house on 23rd and Jackson Streets. Maureen is the oldest, one year older than Jackie.

After Tito and Jermaine came Latoya, and after Marlon and Michael came Randy and Janet.

No one in the Jackson family escaped being musical. Their mother Katherine played clarinet and sang blues and has always enjoyed music. It was their father, though, who had the greatest influence on the children's music.

In 1951 Joe Jackson started playing guitar and singing with the Falcons, a group from Chicago. The group would play mostly blues at colleges and bars. The Falcons often practiced at the Jackson house, and the children watched and listened. The family was never lacking in instruments.

With a large family to support, Joe worked as a crane operator during the week. On weekends he'd have time for his music. He said, "I always wanted to be in entertainment."

Joe always encouraged the musical interest he noticed in his children. At first it was just the three older sons — Jackie, Tito and Jermaine — singing and dancing in the bedroom, pretending they were the Temptations. As their dad saw they were serious about their music jams, he quit the Falcons and gave more of his time to encouraging his children's music.

Often the whole family would jam together — Maureen on violin, Latoya on clarinet, Jermaine doing lead singing, Tito playing guitar and Jackie singing and dancing.

Finally Marlon and Michael joined the group. When Michael was 4, the group won a talent show at Roosevelt High. In the next two years the Jackson Five won nearly all the talent shows around the city. It didn't surprise Joe who said, "You see, we were trying awfully hard."

One of the first places where Michael recalls performing was at a hospital at Christmas time. Being only 4 at the time, all he remembers is that there was a big Santa Claus there.

In 1965 when Michael was 5 and Jackie was 13, the Jackson Five played at a Gary, Indiana bar. They were to receive $8 for the performance; but the audience went wild when they saw Michael, this small version of James Brown, slip and slide all over the stage. The people in the crowd collected more than $100 for the Jackson Five's scheduled $8 performance.

Joe and Katherine Jackson were careful about the way they raised their sons, especially after they began to win talent shows and gain some fame. The parents were careful about the boys' getting "swell-headed."

Joe never let his sons forget that they were just like anybody else. They were never allowed to hang out in the streets. Practice was stressed, and education was valued even before their music. It often bothered Katherine that when there wasn't much money, her husband would still buy more instruments.

Joe and Katherine laugh about this worry now, but Joe appreciated the concern it caused his wife. "When a woman is a good mother and finds all the money going into instruments, she doesn't like it," he said to an interviewer. Still, the Jacksons knew how to live very economically.

Joe Jackson kept on coaching the boys. He would go out to see other groups perform and get ideas for dance and movement. He decided on the arrangement: Jackie in the middle; Tito and Jermaine at the ends with their guitars; and Marlon and Michael on the wing tips. The boys' voices had a natural blend since they were all from one family.

Once the Jackson Five were discovered by Diana Ross and started at Motown Records, their time became more precious. Security had to be very strict to protect them from outsiders. This was especially difficult for the older Jacksons. At a time when most boys get a little freedom from home-life, Jackie and Tito would always have to be home with their younger brothers. They missed out on clubs, dating and many other teen-age activities.

Studio work was not all that easy either. Tito said, ''Sometimes we like to go, sometimes not. Repeating songs over and over — that's a drag, man. It's hard.''

Fans are often one of the J-5's biggest problems. All the Jacksons are personable, out-going people. They like to stop and talk with fans and sign autographs. But security has limited that a great deal. Fans grab at them, pull at their shirt sleeves. So after most appearances, the J-5 are whisked away in waiting limousines.

Success brought the Jackson family to Hollywood Hills. But because the family's practice sessions could be heard throughout the valley, they moved to a sprawling, stucco house in Encino, California.

On the property around the Jackson house are a guesthouse, a playhouse and servants' quarters. Since there are only 6 bedrooms in the house, Marlon, Michael and Randy triple up in one. The other brothers also share.

There are walkways around the house, beautiful grounds, a swimming pool, a badminton court, a basketball half court and an archery range. Inside there is a pool table in a sunken recreation room. Recently Mr. Jackson had a studio built with 16-track equipment for the boys to use in recording.

Jermaine explained why the boys had to switch from public to private school. "So many kids kept cutting school to come over and get our autographs," he said. The Jackson Five had no freedom to move around. The school had to have its telephone changed several times because kids would call asking to speak to Michael.

The Jackson Five grew up enjoying the same things other kids their age do — basketball, dancing, TV, cartoons, pool, cars, pillow fights and card games.

According to Road Manager Tony Jones, stardom hasn't changed the Jackson Five very much. They are aware of themselves and their accomplishments, but they haven't become big-headed. They are a well organized, disciplined group. Each brother appears to know his responsibility to the group, and each one can take care of himself.

Randy, whose contribution may change the group's name to the Jackson Six, plays conga drums and sings. In 1973 when the J-5 were on tour in Europe, Randy made a big hit with his dancing. Applause continued all during his conga drum solo.

Mr. Jackson still remains a big influence on both the musical and personal lives of his sons. As their father and manager, he watches over them very carefully. Jackson helps his sons through the difficulties of being professional at a young age. And, as the Jackson Five grow up, both Katherine and Joe help the boys to maintain their personal lives. "I have tried to teach them to associate with everybody because all people are the same. The only difference is, maybe some got a lucky break."

Sigmund Esco Jackson is called Jackie by everybody. Born on May 4, 1951, Jackie is the oldest and tallest of the Jackson Five. He is 5'10½", and says he'd like to play basketball like Wilt Chamberlain and be able to sing like Robert Goulet. If Jackie isn't playing basketball, he's swimming in the family's pool or riding around Encino Valley in his sports car or on his motorbike.

That's the flashy, athletic side of Jackie Jackson. Jackie is also a serious, business-like person. He studied business administration in college. Jackie says that, when he retires from show business, he'd like to be a businessman. It seems, too, that he is the son most interested in taking over the financial responsibility of the J-5 group. Magazine reporters have called Jackie the "planner" and the "spokesman."

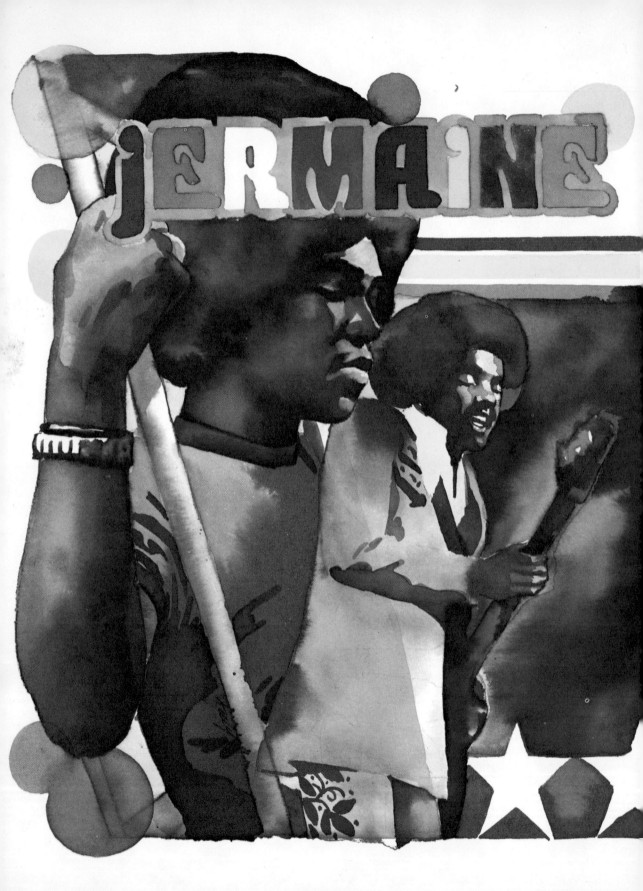

Jackie follows through on his interests. He went to music school to learn to read and write music, to get his musical ideas together. He is also interested in acting. Jackie would like to act in a love story but feels that because of his athletic ability and build he will probably do an athletic role first.

The success of the J-5 has brought Jackie many rewards. An easy, outgoing person, Jackie enjoys people. He enjoys it when fans recognize him, and he's never too busy to talk with fans. He's disappointed when people act strange and over-awed when they talk to him. He feels he's just an ordinary person with ordinary brothers.

Jackie had no trouble calling California his home shortly after their move from Gary, Indiana. He didn't dig winters because they kept him indoors. If he could live anywhere in the world, Jackie says he would stay right in California, near the sand and under the sun.

Since the Jackson Five became popular, it hasn't been unusual to see pictures of Jackie holding a couple of his younger brothers. It's obvious that Jackie has a lot of feeling for his family. "Whenever Mike gets out of line, I beat him up," Jackie laughs as the two wrestle playfully.

Jackie was almost the last of the Five to cut a solo record. It's a smooth, easy-going album with mostly love songs. Jackie has been dating Debbi Foxx, Red Foxx's daughter, as well as other girls; but he says that he doesn't plan to get married for a long time.

It seems that Jackie appreciated the break that he and his brothers got in show business. His ultimate goal in life, he once told a magazine reporter, is to "turn people on for as long as I can in show business, and to help out young brothers and sisters as much as possible."

Tito

"One day, I remember my Dad walking in the door after work and he was carrying something behind his back. It was a guitar! A red one! Man, I was really excited. I'd been fooling with his, and I'd showed him I was serious about playing." Tito was the first of the Jackson Five to pick up an instrument and learn to play it. And the Jackson family credits Tito with the idea of the family's forming a music group.

Toriano Adarryll Jackson, nicknamed Tito, was born October 15, 1953. Tito is proud of his Spanish name and carries the Spanish influence over into his eating. His favorite food is enchiladas.

One reporter for the *Rolling Stone Newspaper* said Tito looked the toughest. He is sturdy and serious, like a Muhammed Ali. Tito keeps his eyes on his guitar and rarely looks out to the audience. Another reporter said that Tito doesn't brag about things. He just does them.

Tito is the mechanic in the family. He loves to tinker with any kind of machine, especially cars. "Grease monkey" is his favorite nickname.

At the same time, Tito is very serious about his music. He sings bass and often plays lead guitar. It isn't unusual to hear Michael cry out on some of their records, "Okay, Tito, you got it." And then the other four support and enjoy Tito's solo on his electric guitar.

Tito learned to play the violin, bass fiddle and saxophone in school. Recently he's learned to play the piano, too. Ever since Tito started playing guitar in 1968, he's used B.B. King and Jimi Hendrix as his models.

Tito is just coming out with his own LP. He says

that it's different from some of the other J-5 stuff. It's "his" kind of music — with more blues and more instrumental pieces from his guitar.

In 1972 Tito became the first of the Jackson Five to marry. A year later, he and his wife, Dee Dee Martes, celebrated the birth of their first child. The son's name sounds familiar, — Toriano Adarryll Jackson II.

Tito is a quiet, uncomplicated person. He looks as though he rejects anything that's phony. He doesn't smile as often and as easily as the other brothers; but when he does smile, it's obvious that Tito Jackson is a warm and caring person.

Jermaine

Quiet, shy, funny, a loner, song-writer, poet, the joker on stage, sex symbol, serious, the cut-up — Jermaine is all of these things. There is no one way to describe Jermaine. He is a person with many different sides who always accepts new challenges.

Jermaine Lajaune Jackson was born December 11, 1954. Like his brothers, he has much respect for his parents and for the way they raised all the kids in the family. "They were pretty strict on us when we were kids," he says. "They told us not to hang out or stay out .... And it paid off!"

For awhile Jermaine always carried around a pet snake. The 4-foot long boa constrictor, named Crusher, would frequently be wrapped around Jermaine's arm as he talked with interviewers.

Unlike Jackie, Jermaine has always liked winter sports. He hopes to take some time to travel and enjoy tobogganing or skiing somewhere in the Alps.

Jermaine started playing guitar when he was 11 before he and his brothers became professionals. He played bass on a guitar before getting a bass guitar. Next he learned to play the piano. Then songwriting became a favorite pastime.

Jermaine has always been very serious about his music. He is going to a special music school, California Arts, to study music theory and composition.

Jermaine often likes to find a place where he can be alone, where he can get his thoughts together. Jermaine enjoys what he calls a "deep thinking mood." That is when he writes songs and poetry.

When he has time, Jermaine hopes to write a book about the Jackson Five's success. Movies are also in Jermaine's future. He is looking forward to acting but also to composing the musical scores for movies. Jermaine plans big; yet he takes the time to think his plans through.

At the end of 1973 Jermaine made public another commitment. On December 15 Jermaine married Hazel Joy Gordy, daughter of Motown's Berry Gordy, at the Beverly Hills Hotel.

Hazel and Jermaine had met 5 years before when the Jackson Five first came to Motown. "There's no cellophane about her," Jermaine says of Hazel; "she's true blue." Similarly, Hazel says, "Jermaine is very honest, and I like honesty." He's a "great companion" with whom Hazel shares many things in common.

Jermaine still spends 4 hours a day rehearsing with his brothers for concerts, records, TV shows and tours. Hazel keeps busy while Jermaine is on the road. She plans to study real estate or open an antique shop when she is finished with her courses in interior design.

When Jermaine makes solo albums, the sound is definitely different from the whole Jackson Five sound. His voice is soft, and he often chooses mellow songs to record. Many have said he sounds like Smokey Robinson, especially on ballads.

There's a variation in the background sounds to Jermaine's songs — some with steel guitar sounds, others with vocal harmonies. Jermaine's albums are examples of a young man on the move toward becoming a complete professional.

Marlon

"Sometimes when my brothers are rehearsing in the studio," Latoya Jackson says, "I'll go in and watch them work out new dance numbers and steps. Marlon will pull me up, and together we will do a new dance step. He really is a great dancer as well as my other brothers; but Marlon just seems to have a magic touch for dancing."

Early in 1974 reporters were saying that Marlon is the Jackson to watch. He seems ready to emerge as a talented solo perfomer, very much a part of the Five, but also an individual in his own right.

Marlon David Jackson was born on March 12, 1957. At home he shares a room with Michael and Randy, and likes to swim, play basketball and pool. He has recently become interested in electronics.

When asked what part Marlon plays in the harmonics of the Five, somebody said, "Marlon blows a mean doo-wop." Marlon doesn't sing lead, but he does like to grab the microphone and add whoops at the end of the songs. And Marlon is considered the most professional dancer of the group.

MARLON

With Jermaine married, Latoya says she spends more time with Marlon and Michael. Marlon has his driver's license and is always willing to take Latoya wherever she needs to go.

Marlon's sign is Pisces, but he says he doesn't believe in astrology because he feels there are only half-truths there. Marlon seems to like to think for himself. He's been called his own man.

Michael and Marlon get into the scuffles that most brothers do — over wearing each other's clothes or whose turn it is to do dishes. But it seems that arguments don't linger too long with Marlon. He's quick to make up. Marlon has been referred to as "the lovable one."

Marlon is considered the quietest of the Jackson Five. He seems to be comfortable with who he is now and is not afraid to wait for the right time to display all that he has to offer. As one reporter noted, "Marlon is as visible as any corner of a polished diamond."

Michael

Michael Joe Jackson, the youngest of the Jackson Five, has been out in front of the group singing lead for as long as the brother-team has been popular. Large round eyes set in a round face under a round Afro make Michael a very pleasing person to watch. It is also pleasing to watch his professional command of the stage in both singing and dancing.

Michael was born on August 29, 1958, and began singing with his brothers when he was four. Before long Michael proved to be a born mimic. He learned to imitate James Brown. Michael knew every turn, twist, jerk and angle in the James Brown routine at the microphone.

In fact, Motown's stage coordinator for the J-5 said later that it was difficult to steer Michael away from that style.

Michael is what show business people call a "natural," a pro on stage and a down-to-earth kid off stage. Many magazine and newspaper interviewers comment on how Michael doesn't hog the attention or come on too strong, but he's not afraid to show his best self on stage. And Michael fits right back into the rest of the family when the spotlights are off.

Michael is definitely not a loner. He never travels alone and stays pretty close to home. He enjoys taking photographs with the camera Diana Ross gave him. Watching TV cartoons is relaxing for him, and he likes to make some of his own cartoon sketches. Throughout their hotel stays on tours, Michael has been known to be very good at pillow fighting.

Michael's musical abilites keep growing as he grows. He has learned to play both drums and piano, and he's not afraid of practice. It takes Michael 2 hours to record a song. First he sings his part and goes over it many times until it's right. Then the other Jacksons do their part behind Michael's voice.

Michael was the first to make a solo LP. "Ben" and "Music and Me" stand out among Michael's hits. Michael's albums show both a soft, mellow side and a hard, bouncy side.

Michael has grown up with a strange hobby. He's a grocery store nut. He loves to wander up and down the aisles of different grocery stores.

Like the other Jacksons, Michael has talent. His voice and musical pacing have the beginnings of a true professional. It's up to Michael now to see just how he works out his gifts as he matures.

JACKSON FIVE
CARLY SIMON
BOB DYLAN
JOHN DENVER
THE BEATLES
ELVIS PRESLEY
JOHNNY CASH
CHARLEY PRIDE
ARETHA FRANKLIN
ROBERTA FLACK
STEVIE WONDER

Rock'n PopStars